Newton Ferrers and Noss Mayo Remembered

Arthur L. Clamp

A Season's Greeting Card

The *Kitley Belle*, close to Pope's Quay, forms the centrepiece to this card dated before 1914 showing Noss Creek at about half tide with Newton Ferrers in the background. The Brook runs into the water there where one of the village drinking taps was situated. The various boats in the foreground were used for getting around the estuary, light fishing and racing in the annual regatta.

This version of the book is virtually as originally published.
There are now additional pages at the back providing information about the author.

The republishing project is being managed by Arthur's grandson, Steven Gibson. We aim to find all the research that he was involved in publishing, preserving it for the next generation as part of 'The Clamp Collection'.

INTRODUCTION

The two villages of Newton Ferrers and Noss Mayo have undergone considerable changes during the past sixty years and more so much so that the once traditional ways of making a livelihood from the sea and land have also gone. The appearances of both villages have also changed from groups of cottages hugging the water's edge with a few isolated houses and farms looking down from nearby high land to quite large developments of pre and post-war private dwellings and a change in use of old buildings standing along the creeks.

This illustrated booklet tries to place on record a permanent assembly of the many once common scenes along and around the very beautiful Yealm estuary with its once popular ferries taking people to and from Steer Point to catch the trains into Plymouth.

This title is not meant to be a comprehensive account of the growth of the locality or to examine the reasons why changes have taken place. These, it can be said in passing, have been mainly influenced by communications becoming more efficient and fast than was the case years ago. Undoubtedly the car has been the main factor in bringing about these changes which places both villages within easy reach of Plymouth.

Newton Ferrers and Noss Mayo, although seen by the visitor as one locality, have been and still are quite distinct villages with many families associating themselves with one or other and in the annual regatta the opportunity has not been missed in friendly competition between both. The villages are in separate parishes with their own churches, with Noss Mayo's former building still standing in part ruin at Stoke Beach, public houses, post offices, schools and few shops. Some of the scenes in this booklet will show aspects of these and the separate fishing and crabbing activities which was once a feature of these tidal waters. The many leisure boats and yachts of today moor on waters once rowed and sailed across by smaller and less expensive craft from which local men made their living by fishing and crabbing in nearby waters. Others went further out and, from time to time, fishermen from France would call using, like the estuarymen, the baulking stores built by Lord Revelstoke for handling and packing catches. All that is now gone apart from photographic records and memories.

Likewise major changes have taken place that rendered the ferries unprofitable and although owned and run by local people, with many others visiting the Yealm, their demise came after the closure of the Yealmpton railway and the increase in car ownership. Their period of useful service spanned about five decades the first appearing on the Yealm just before the turn of the century when Mr. James Ford from Plymouth started developing the area overlooking the pool and building the well known Yealm Hotel. Then it was quite a difficult task to reach this area from Plymouth. It was really the opening of the railway to Yealmpton in 1898 which started the changes.

A longer innings can be marked up by the lifeboat. Three boats saw service on the Yealm station from 1878 to 1927 and although there was only four rescues or assistances many local men served the boats faithfully and, sometimes, at risk to themselves. The lifeboat house is still standing and is a happy reminder of the care expressed for mariners in distress on local waters.

An earlier era comes to mind when one sees the old coastguard cottages almost facing the Yealm Hotel. In the early days of the last century it was considered to be a gainful occupation in bringing in goods without paying custom and, no doubt, this supplemented from time to time, the generally meagre earnings of most people of the area. The pattern is much the same along the whole of the south coast.

A close look at both villages today will reveal many reminders of what the fabric and structure was before the developments of recent decades. The Victorian reading rooms are still in use, the villge schools are still standing, with Newton's in use although Noss's, with the date 1839 engraved on it, being put to occasional other uses. The chapel and churches can also rightly claim a long lineage in the lives of many families and their numerous wall monuments, which deserve a study in themselves, are apt reminders of once well known people, events and tragedies such as those listed lost during both world wars.

In my enquiries references were made about particular people and I wish these to be mentioned. There was Bill Roach, the ferryman, William West, the stonemason whose skill is still evident in many existing walls, the Hodge brothers and their ownership of the ferries, Harry Hockaday, fisherman and onetime lifeboat coxswain and the Fosters, fishermen and postmasters. There are many, many more which deserve further study and recording.

It is hoped that the illustrations reproduced between these covers will bring back memories of past days and activities and show how both villages have changed over the years.

Nowadays the locality is home for many retired and professional people; there is a very active Yealm Yacht Club, the woodlands still give pleasure to walkers and the wildlife of the estuary warrants close viewing during all seasons of the year.

Acknowledgments

I am indebted to many people for suggesting that a booklet of this kind be produced for the area and this was only possible by the kind loan of photographs and postcards by Mr. R. West, Mr. J. Stribling, Mr. A. Kittridge and others with support from various libraries and their staff. Other photographs have been loaned to me since the publication of this title and I would welcome others in the hope that another illustrated booklet could be made up in a year or two's time.

Arthur L. Clamp,
203 Elburton Road,
Plymouth, Devon PL9 8HX

The Albert Steam Boat

The decorated boat in the background may show that it is regatta day and the *Albert* steam boat has come out from Plymouth, owned by the Saltash and Devonport Steamship Co., with many passengers for the occasion. The year is thought to be 1901 and the vessel is probably being used as a grandstand to the various water activities.

The Yam Yam

This was the very unusual name of the boat seen here about 1899. It was probably an ex-Admiralty steam pinnace owned by Mr. James Ford who built the Yealm Hotel the previous year and used the boat for bringing people out from Plymouth via the railway halt at Steer Point. The circular undercroft of the hotel held oil-driven engines for emergency lighting.

The Yealm Hotel

This was built as part of the development of the area by James Ford who purchased the land from Lord Revelstoke of Membland. The date of this postcard must be about 1901 when the wooden jetty was in regular use by passengers landing from the daily ferries from Steer Point. On this day many people must have been attracted here by a special event which could have been the regatta.

Springfield Cottage 1937

The view is from Back Road, Noss Mayo, and shows the bungalow built for Mr. William J. Lapthorne in the late 1920s. Water was piped into the house from a nearby spring hence the name. Many later houses now overlook the estuary where the isolated police house stands on the far bank close to the old footpath now made up to form Church Park Road.

Riverside Road West

This late 1930's view of Newton's waterfront shows the different houses and buildings that now make up the familiar hillside layout. Then the buildings were new, others had been renovated and the church is no longer standing by itself on the hill.

Riverside Road East about 1906

The slipway runs down to the foreshore overlooked by Honeysuckle Cottage, home of Mr. and Mrs. Shepherd for many years, with the thatched cottage beyond the tree where Mr. Sam Derry lived. The date is about 1906 and part of Noss Mayo can be seen in the background on the right. The once familiar tree was cut down many years ago.

Motor Vessel Pioneer at Pope's Quay

The two upper views on this page show the new motor vessel *Pioneer* which came into service during the latter half of the 1920s replacing the long serving paddle steamers. Both pictures were taken from Point, Noss Mayo, showing the *Swan Inn*, the old thatched post office and the present one opposite at the bottom of Pillory Hill. The boat was bought at St. Mawes, Cornwall, and did service in the Yealm waters until the mid-1930s when it was left as a hulk to break up in Noss Creek. The various other boats moored at half tide were used for getting around the estuary, fishing and probably some crabbing. The post office was run by George H. Foster.

Bridgend from Noss Church

This 1930s view captures the small locality before it was surrounded with many buildings. Crown Yealm House is on its own facing Bridgend Quay and Junket Corner. Beyond the quay is the old malthouse with its long roof and the thick woods overlook the narrow valley which has been known to flood at times of very high tides.

Mrs. Ellen West

This pre-1914 photograph shows her outside her cottage on West View Hill from where local newspapers were sold, bread and other items. She lost her fisherman husband at sea and brought up a family of eight children on her own. The newspaper boards show the two main Plymouth papers — the *Western Morning News* and the *Western Daily Mercury* which ceased production in 1921.

Holy Cross Church and Vicarage

Various members of the Yonge family from Puslinch were vicars here from 1752 to 1938, apart from one or two small breaks, and they were also squires as well. This 1906 view shows the vicarage then occupied by the Rev. Charles B. Yonge, M.A., and, on the front lawn and field, many parties and social events have taken place in connection with the life of the church and village.

West View, Newton Hill

Mrs. Ellen West is here with her friend Miss Bessie Phillips but the gentleman with the cigarette in his mouth has not been recognised. The thatched cottage is now Newton Ferrers post office but then it was a private dwelling.

Turning Around

The once familiar *Kitley Belle* turns by Newton Ferrers in readiness to land passengers for tea and an opportunity to explore the area. Timings for the ferries were often governed by the state of the tide; in some cases the ferry was not able to reach the higher landing stages.

Kitley Belle at the Jetty

A very crowded boat with another, which appears to be in tow, is captured in 1905 picture which was likely to have been taken place on a regatta day. Other people line the waterfront and, to the right, is a large house boat decorated for the occasion. The old coastguard cottages are on the hillside behind.

View of River Yealm

The sloping gardens of the coastguards are in the immediate foreground in this view of the river at the turn of the century. Thorn House can be seen once the home of William Arkwright, then Mrs. Robert Sebag-Montefiore, later Stanley E. Gerald, M.S., F.R.C.S. round the time this view was taken.

Arriving for Passengers

The year is about 1905 and the *Kitley Belle* is here on Noss creek to take or bring passengers to and from Steer Point. The crew were George Hodge, skipper, Ernest Hodge, engineer, George Hodge, junior, deck hand and Elliot Hodge, general helper. The tower of St. Peter's Revelstoke dominates the village.

Homeguard Inspection

The local "Dad's Army" is on parade outside of Holy Cross church sometime in 1940 being inspected by Lady Astor accompanied by the Rev. C. H. D. Grimes. In the ranks are recognised Mr. G. Thorn and Mr. B. Baker and Lt. H. Kingcombe. No doubt others will be identified and memories of these days easily recalled.

Newton Creek View

This expansive view of the locality hides the much smaller Noss Creek to the left but clearly shows the undeveloped land running down to the main creek with the Yealm Hotel in the far distance. The date is about 1906; St. Peters is in the foreground and Newton village is on the right lower side.

Noss Creek in the opening years of this century.

Motor Vessel Pioneer

Here she is at Steer Point with George Hodge, Junior, assisting a passenger aboard who alighted from the train at Steer Point Halt sometime in the late 1920s. This engine-driven vessel replaced the former paddle steamers whose running proved too costly by increases in coal prices as a result of the general strike of 1926. She finished her days as a hulk on Noss beach in the mid-1930s.

Princess Royal Paddle Steamer, about 1910

It is thought that passengers are being transferred to the *Kitley Belle* to be taken to Steer Point and then back to Plymouth to complete a circular tour from Plymouth. In front of her are crabbing boats owned by local fishermen. The day's outing from and to Plymouth by steamer and train was very popular especially on Bank holidays.

Last Visit

This records the last visit of the paddle steamer *Alexandra* in September, 1927, withdrawn with others of its kind because of the increasing costs of coal and the coming of petrol driven engines. She was built in 1888 and was then scrapped at Cattedown having completed 40 years of service. Boats are taking off passengers in the Pool.

Betwixt two Church Towers

These stand above the relatively undeveloped hillsides in this view thought to be dated about 1910. In the far distance is *Hewster's* Quarry and below it, at the waterline, is Bridgend Quay behind which stood the malthouse. Nearer on the left are the small quays for the fishing boats with Riverside Road West's cottages and gardens running down to the creek. Note one of the *Greyback* boats beached on the right and raced in the annual regatta.

Bert West, Postmaster

It looks very much that he is posing here for a visiting photographer sometime in the 1930s; also in view is a large house boat moored below Point House. Noss Creek is still only overlooked by a few houses and many boats are moored along its shore.

Noss Mayo Omnibus

An early 1930's bus can be seen here parked outside of the Tilly Institute close to the former village school which was opened in 1839. The chapel is just visible on the left and the *Globe Inn* to the right slightly out of picture. Regular bus services to Plymouth started in the 1920s.

Crossing the Pool

The bowler-hatted gentleman has not been recognised but it looks very much that the ferry is being prepared to take him and his lady across the Pool. Note the pads on the side of the rear boat and the very large house boat moored in deep water. The picture is in front of Ferry Cottage.

Regatta Day, August, about 1910

The spirit of the festive occasion is captured in this very early photograph showing the *Princess Royal* paddle passenger steamer behind the funnel of which can just be seen the smaller *Kitley Girl* steamer. The two boats in the foreground are a Plymouth hooker (see the registration number) and a house boat named *Lamorna*. Races appear to be in progress in the background to the left.

Awaiting Passengers at Pope's Quay

The pre-1914 scene shows the well-remembered *Kitley Belle* passenger steamer waiting for people wishing to go into Plymouth via the railway halt at Steer Point. This was the top most terminus when the tide was right. A crabbing boat is by the old boat store and the hill with few houses remains undeveloped.

Noss Creek at nearly High Tide

This pre-1914 view shows fishermen's boats at their moorings, single-masted and worked with oars. The larger beach boat is a *Greyback* and was kept for the regatta races and worked by four oarsmen and a coxswain. The view is from Point View showing Newton Ferrers in the left background and Noss Mayo on the right with the thatched post office and the old boathouse at the water's edge. Mr. R. West recalls Bill Clark, a fisherman, living in the cottages at Newton with his store in front where crab pots were made.

Local Competition

The level of competition between the various Plymouth based ferry companies was such that one company's boat would follow another as seen here passing the then isolated Yealm Hotel. The forward vessel is the *Hibernia*, owned by the Millbrook Steamboat Co., and the nearer is the *Princess Royal* owned by the Saltash Three Towns Steamboat Co. They are going up to the tea gardens.

Returning to Plymouth

Still in hot pursuit but now coming down the main estuary of the Yealm, they are on their way back passing one house boat moored near the lifeboat station. Both pictures were taken on the same day. There was a limited passenger traffic on the waters around Plymouth and competition for it went on ceaselessly for years with all kinds of offers to induce people to take different boats.

Returning to Plymouth

This scene of the Yealm estuary taken from near Rocket Cottage showing the paddle steamer passenger boat *Alexandra* returning after an enjoyable excursion into this estuary. The Mewstone is in the distance and the ferry was a familiar sight until 1927. The photograph is thought to have been taken about 1920.

Kiln Quay about 1912

Tea gardens provided refreshments for passengers out from Plymouth for the day as seen here landing from the paddle steamer *Alexandra*. The house itself could accommodate boats moored underneath it.

Looking from Wembury Point

This magnificent view of Newton Creek, the boats and buildings, shows the locality at its best sometime between the wars. Many features will be easily identified from the Yealm Hotel, lifeboat station to other features further up the creek. Note the boat in the foreground covered over for living and the relative emptiness of the Pool to that of today.

Riverside Road West

This between the wars view has not radically changed although the tree has long gone and some alterations can be quickly spotted at Noss in the far distance. The thatched cottage is the last along here but in the background an electric cable pole shows that lighting has reached the villages by the time this view was taken.

Ferry Cottage

This 1906 view probably shows the cottage and small thatched building in their original state where charges for the ferry were made according to the list on the renovated board now on display. The crossing was to Warren Point or the jetty below the Yealm Hotel and the path shown here led towards Mouthstone Point.

Living on the Water

From time to time various people had boats partly converted to allow them to live on them normally during the summer months. Various boats can be seen in this booklet with part of their cabins enclosed as shown here sometime between 1925 and 1930. The old lifeboat house was still in use then and the jetty running down alongside it was the landing point for passengers from the railway and ferries and for visitors out from Plymouth for the day on steamer trips.

Summer Visitors to the Locality

This 1930s scene (note the bonnets of the ladies in the boat) is not much different from today with buildings occupying almost all the hillsides. The *Dolphin Inn's* roof has been slated, the school and policeman's house now stand in the former field and it is the time of the year when the ferrymen are at their busiest taking visitors from one side of the creek to the other.

St. Peter the Poor Fisherman

This now derelict church overlooking Stoke beach was severely damaged in a storm in April, 1868, and was replaced by the present church at Noss Mayo a few years later. The ivy seen here has been removed and some renovation to the walls and roof has taken place over the past few years. The font is still there and two Georgian wall boards listing the commandments.

Riverside Road East

A little girl with her dog view with some interest what appears to be the baker's van in the distance presumably loading with bread from the bakehouse sometime in the 1930s. Bill Roach's cottage is to the left just below road level and well beyond is the men's reading room where snooker and cards are played. It would be interesting to be able to identify the people halfway along this road.

Riverside Road West

Some local children are quite curious at the visiting photographer when this view was taken around 1906. One child is thought to be Sidney West. Note the heavy boots they are all wearing! The two cottages are named Glen and Virginia. Apart from one or two superficial changes this view had not changed very much over the years.

The Old Post Office

Has the mail just arrived from Yealmpton at Bridgend for delivery to nearby houses? This 1908 scene looks very much like it showing possibly Bert West in the group outside the well-signed post office. The paraffin street lamp on the left was lit daily by Mr. West behind which stands a very pleasant thatched summer house.

Low Tide at Bridgend

The roadside horse trough will probably be well remembered fed by water from the stream coming down from the Membland area past Post Office farm standing on the high side of the small road bridge. This was run by Mr. Hingston and his two sons.

Bridgend in 1905

This very early postcard view of the locality recalls the days when almost all the hillsides running down to the estuary were not built upon. In the distance is Pear Tree Cottage with one other building, although the farm on the left was still a going concern. The trough can be seen but the buildings on the right were later to be changed to those of present days.

Recasting of Bells

This took place in 1957 when a new bell frame was also made for Holy Cross Church. Here they can be seen in front of the entrance and the work was undertaken by a company at Loughborough and funds were raised by Rev. C. H. D. Grimes. Six bells were renewed and they were first pealed by the bellringers under the captaincy of Mrs. Morton.

Hand Bell-Ringers

The new year is being heralded in by these bell ringers at Castle De Rio in Court Woods in the late 1950s. The team is led by Reg. West supported by Ted Goodland, Bob Hurrell, Roy Foster, Ted Furzeland and Norman Ellis. They gave various demonstrations of their playing to raise funds for the costs of maintaining the church bells at different places and events in the area.

Panoramic View 1901

Two photographs have been butted together to form this unique record of the land and waterside facing the estuary before it was developed in the first decades of this century. Moving from left to right can be seen the flagpole in front of the old coastguard cottages, Thorn House away in the distance, a lime kiln and cottages, the steamer, thought to be the *Albert*, farmland known locally as Mr. Moon's estate, cottages and the lifeboat station which was built in 1877-8 housing three lifeboats, the *Bowman*, *Daring* and *Michael Smart* during the years it was used. Then there is the Yealm Hotel built in 1898 with its jetty below and finally a large wall stands prominently to the right with three isolated houses on the skyline.

From a 1901 Book:

"The inhabitants are chiefly engaged on the building operations and development of *The River Yealm Building Estate* purchased from the late Lord Revelstoke of Membland, by that well-known estate developer Mr. James Ford of Plymouth. Yealm can be reached by sea, three quarter of an hour's time, by train to Steer Point or Yealmpton and then by boat down river. There is an annual regatta here each year."

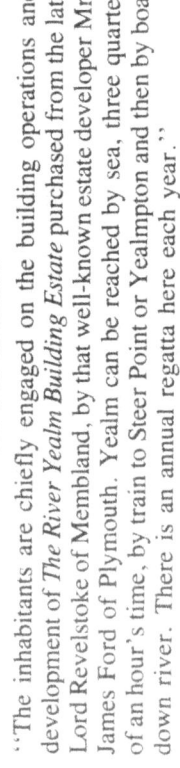

Pope's Quay about 1901

Another postcard view of these buildings overlooking the narrow Noss creek which can be crossed at low water on the *Voss* or slightly raised walkway over the mud. At least one of the boats shown appears to be a crabber with its single mast.

Interior of Holy Cross Church

This view of the interior shows the old chairs which were later replaced by the present oak pews. The date is around 1905 and oil lamps can be seen suspended from the roof. The Rev. Charles B. Yonge, M.A., was the vicar at this period.

St. Peter's Church Revelstoke

The tower and church almost stand alone in open fields overlooking the estuary with Newton Ferrers to the right. The church was consecrated in September, 1882, by the Bishop of Exeter having been built mainly at the expense of Mr. Edward Baring of Membland. The architect was Mr. Giles St. Aubyn and the year this view was recorded was about 1901.

Trade Directories of 1926

This annual book listing most of the people in an area and describing part of its background can be a source of much interesting information. These for 1926 give a good picture of both localities in that year.

REVELSTOKE is a parish, on the south coast in Bigbury bay, 3 miles south from Yealmpton station on a branch from Plymouth, and 10 south-west from Ivybridge station on the South Devon section of the main line of the Great Western railway, 10 south-east from Plymouth and 9 south from Plympton; it is in the Tavistock division of the county, hundred of Plympton, petty sessional division of Ermington and Plympton, union of Plympton St. Mary, county court district of Plymouth, rural deanery of Plympton, archdeaconry of Plymouth and diocese of Exeter. This place, since 1885, has afforded the title of baron to a branch of the Baring family. The church of St. Peter, built in 1882, by Edward, 1st Lord Revelstoke, at a cost of £29,000, from designs by Mr. J. P. St. Aubyn, architect, is an edifice of stone in the Perpendicular style, and consists of chancel, nave, aisles, south porch and an embattled western tower containing a clock with chimes and 8 bells; the seats, executed by Hems, of Exeter, are of solid oak handsomely carved, each bearing a different device; the font and the piers of the arcades are of granite; the stained west window was presented by the parishioners and the side windows of the chancel by the Rev. H. F. Roe M.A. rector 1871-89, and there are several in the south aisle to the Baring family, including one added in 1893, in memory of the late Louisa Emily Charlotte (Bultcel), wife of Edward, 1st Baron Revelstoke, who died 16 October, 1892, and one to Edward Charles, 1st Lord Revelstoke, himself: in the chancel is a triptych, representing "The Nativity" and "The Annunciation;" the vestry is under the north transept; there are 250 sittings. The ancient and ivy-clad church of St. Peter, situated near Stoke Point close to the sea, is now in ruins, but since 1873 a portion has been repaired, at a cost of £800. The register dates from the year 1054. The living is a rectory, net yearly value £500, and residence, in the gift of the Bishop of Exeter, and held since 1923 by the Rev. Edward Ernest Benson M.A. of Oxford University. There is a Wesleyan chapel; there is a reading room and library containing about 600 volumes, mostly presented by Lord Revelstoke. The population is chiefly at Noss Mayo, on the side of a creek adjacent to the mouth of the river Yealm and opposite to Newton Ferrers. Mr. Stanley Pitts is lord of the manor. The soil is sandy; subsoil, mixed. The chief crops are wheat, barley and roots. The area is 1,544 acres of land, 7 of tidal water and 124 of foreshore; rateable value, £1,422; the population in 1921 was 446.

Sexton, William Hall.

Post Office, Noss Mayo.—George Henry Foster, sub-postmaster. Letters arrive through Plymouth. The nearest money order & telegraph office is at Newton Ferrers

Public Elementary School (mixed), built in 1839, for 200 children; Miss Lankester, mistress

---

NEWTON FERRERS is a parish and village, pleasantly seated on an eminence on the north of a navigable creek which runs into the river Yealm and nearly 2 miles from the sea coast, 3 south from Yealmpton station on the line from Plymouth to Yealmpton, 8 south from Plympton station on the South Devon section of the Great Western railway, 7½ south-east from Plymouth and 9 south-west from Ivybridge; it is in the Tavistock division of the county, hundred of Ermington, petty sessional division of Ermington and Plympton, union of Plympton St. Mary, county court district of Plymouth, rural deanery of Plympton, archdeaconry of Plymouth and diocese of Exeter. The church of the Holy Cross is an edifice of stone, chiefly in the Perpendicular style, consisting of chancel, nave, aisles, south porch with carved wagon roof and an embattled western tower, containing a clock and 6 bells; there are several monuments in the church to the Potter and Yonge families, and memorial windows to the Rev. John Yonge B.A. rector from 1812, and to the Rev. Duke Yonge M.A. rector 1877-82, to whom also a marble and alabaster reredos has been erected as a memorial; the new oak parclose screens, and a font of veined alabaster were executed by Mr. Harry Hems, of Exeter; the church was restored in 1886, at a cost of £4,400, and affords 300 sittings. The register dates from the year 1599. The living is a rectory, net yearly value £577, including 88 acres of glebe, in the gift of John Yonge esq. B.A., J.P. and held since 1891 by the Rev. Charles Burell Yonge M.A. of Keble College, Oxford. St. Mary's chapel, a private chapel attached to Gnaton Hall, which is the property of Lt.-Col. Joshua Craven-Hoyle T.D., D.L., J.P. was built in 1886 at a cost of about £3,500, and is an edifice of stone in the Gothic style, from designs by G. H. F. Prynne, architect, consisting of chancel, nave and north porch: a dado of coloured Devonshire marble runs round the interior; the triptych is of carved oak; the screen, pulpit and the lectern are of brass, beautifully wrought; the font is of Caen stone with marble shafts; on the walls of the nave and in the passage way from the house to the church are paintings on oak of scriptural subjects by Mr. E. A. F. Prynne, let into the walls; the chapel affords 74 sittings. There is a lifeboat station. Lt. Col. Joshua Craven-Hoyle T.D., D.L., J.P. is lord of the manor of Newton; John Yonge esq. B.A., J.P. is lord of the manor of Puslinch. John Yonge esq. and Lt.-Col. Joshua Craven-Hoyle are the principal land owners. The soil is chiefly clay; subsoil, rock. The chief crops are wheat, oats, barley and roots. The area is 3,325 acres of land, 1 of water, 36 of tidal water and 133 of foreshore; rateable value, £7,679; the population in 1921 was 772 in the civil parish and 755 in the ecclesiastical parish.

TORR, about 3 miles north-east, is in this parish. There is a Church of England mission room, to seat about 100; also a Wesleyan chapel with 250 seats, built in 1909 at a cost of £1,200; attached is a school for 140 children.

Post, M. O., T. & T. E. D. Office.—Mrs. Eliza C. Phipps, sub-postmistress. Letters should have Devon added

Public Elementary School (mixed & infants), built in 1874, for 100 children; Miss Ethel H. Ainley, mistress

Police Station, Archibald Harding, constable in charge

Conveyance.—Motor omnibuses to & from Plymouth several times daily

Carriers to Plymouth.—Reginald & Leonard Doddridge, daily at 9 a.m. (motor)

1926

(Marked thus * letters received through Yealmpton.)

PRIVATE RESIDENTS.

(For T N's see general list of Private Residents at end of book.)

*Andrews Wm. Hy. Lanherne, Torr
Bensted-Smith William Francis M.B
Broadhurst Lt.-Commdr. John Rd. R.N. (ret.), Seaview
Ching Sidney James, Hendra
Cooper Paymaster-Capt. Wilfrid R.N. (ret.), Yealm cottage
*Crago Fredk. Wm. Wood-side Torr
*Ford William George, Trelawney villa, Torr
Frazer Percy Douglas, The Towers
*Huddy Geo. Kenwyn, Torr
Hamerton William Aubrey Bennett, Batang Kali
Hinde George d'Arcy, Innisfree
Holmes à Court Hon. Mrs. Henry Worsley, Rose cottage
*Jack Charles, Cheviot lodge, Torr
Kidwell William George, Riverside
Kingcombe Wm. Hy. Ellis, Ainslie
Kingcombe The Misses, Haw's Park
*Laptain Charles Henry, St. Andrew's lodge, Torr
Lapthorn Herbert T. Laburnum
La Trobe Miss, The Nook
*Leaman Walter Theodore, Allington, Torr
Land Fras. shopkpr
*Lane Wm. dairyman, Torr
Lapthorne Herbt. Jn. shopkpr
Lister Jn. farmer, Creacombe
Manwell Wm. Hy. shopkpr
Newton Ferrers & Noss Mayo Women's Institute (Mrs. W. Cooper, hon. sec)
Newton Ferrers Reading Room (F. Wyatt, hon. sec)
Phillips Henry Joseph Jordan, carpntr
†Plymouth Co-operative Society Ltd. (T N Plymstock 56X1) & farmers, Lambside (T N Yealmpton 19X) & Caulston

*McCready Lt.-Col. Thomas Robert D.S.O., M.C. Trefusis, Torr
McDermott Maj. Arthur William Patrick, Restawhile
*Melrose Malcolm Milton, The Copse, Torr
Mountstephen W. H. The Haven
Northcott Mrs. Braeside
Oakley Charles Fredk. Wycherley
*Oaten Edward Joseph, Boskenna, Torr
Palmer Harry Bennett, Elstow
Pode Miss, Cottage green
Scoble Urban Herman, The Bungalow
Selwood Thomas Deering, Inglewood
Smith Darley Ernest, Horswells
Tanner Mrs. Romsdale
*Wimbush Miss, The Quarry, Torr
*Wood Edwd. Joshua B.A., M.B. Torr ho
*Wood John Craster, Carnethy, Torr
*Woollcombe Maj. Frank R., M.C. Rockdale, Torr
Wright George Henry, Rosemont
Yonge Rev. Charles Burell M.A. (rector)
Yonge Duke Mohun, West park, Torr
*Yonge John B.A., J.P. Puslinch ho
Yonge John Harry, Mewstone cottage
Yonge Mrs. Court house

COMMERCIAL.

Marked thus † farm 150 acres or over.

Barratt Frank & Harry, farmers, Ashton, Torr
*Pope Edwd. head gardener to Lt.-Col. J. Craven-Hoyle T.D., D.L., J.P. Gnaton
*Proctor Edwd. farmer, Cannacombe farm
River Yealm Hotel Ltd. (Hy. Tenney, manager), River Yealm hotel. T N Plymstock 80Y
Roach Geo. Hy. butcher. T N Plymstock 60Y6
*†Rogers Andrew, farmer, Brownstone. T N Yealmpton 16
Seymour Louisa (Miss), shopkpr
Shannon Rd. farmer, Newton farm
Sitters Leonard, carpntr

Bensted-Smith Wm. Fras. M.A., M.B., B.Ch.Camb., M.R.C.S.Eng., L.R.C.P.Lond. (Fox & Bensted-Smith), physcn & surgn. T N Plymstock 56Y1
Bonnie J. (Mrs.), boarding ho Barnicott. T N Plymstock 60X1
Burt Chas. Harry, farmer, Parsonage farm. T N Plymstock 56X3
†Cane Benj. farmer, Preston farm
*Cawse Rt. coal dlr. Torr
*Cole Eustace, farmer, Torr
*Cross Wm. Jas. farmer, Torr. T N Yealmpton 38
Daymond Albert Henry, builder
Doddridge Regnld. & Leonard, carriers. T N Plymstock 60X4
Doddridge Wm. boot repr
†Farley Wm. Jn. & Septimus Boyes, farmers, Lolesbury
Fox & Bensted-Smith, physcns. & surgns
Gill Ernest, farmer, Newton Downs
†Hacker Jn. Dawe, farmer, Broadmore
*Harvey Warwick, farmer, Creber
*Hiskens Geo. Aug. commrcl. travllr. Riverdale, Torr
*Hollow Jn. Fras. motor garage, Torr. T N Yealmpton 6
Hosford Benjamin, Newton farm
Irish Ernest Veale, farmer, Bridgend
Kingcombe Harry, motor car garage
*Toms Arth. Louis, farmer, Wrescombe
*†Toms Fredk. Wm. farmer, Collaton
Tope Archibald, carrier
Tope Wm. boat bldr
Townsend Hy. confctnr. Torr
*Tucker Sidney, road contrctr. Torr
*Tucker Wm. Hy. refresh. rms. Torr
*Uren Rd. farmer, Blowden
West Wm. stone mason
*Wills Maud (Miss), teacher of music, Torr
Worth Harry, Dolphin inn
*Yealmpton Women's Institute (Miss E. Wimbush, hon. sec.), Torr

---

Benson Rev. Edward Ernest M.A (rector), Rectory

COMMERCIAL.

Algate Edward Thomas, boat builder
Andrews Silas (Mrs.), refreshment rms. Noss Mayo. T N Plymstock 60Y5
Banker Nicholas, Swan P.H
Cawse Robert, coal merchant, Bridge end (postal address, Newton Ferrers)

Chaffe Richard Wm. frmr Worswell
Clark Fredk. Jn. butcher, Noss Mayo
Foster George Hy. grocer, Noss Mayo
Hodge Vincent, baker & grocer. T N Plymstock 60Y4
Newton Chas. Globe inn
Paige Stanley, dairyman, Coombe
Parsons Emily (Mrs.) & Son, blcksmths
Parsons Emily (Mrs.), refreshment rooms, Noss Mayo

Plymouth Co-operative Society Ltd. farmers, Netton
Sims Jn. Hy. boat owner, Noss Mayo
Tilly Institute & Library (Geo. Reeves, librarian)
Wakeham John, farmer, Rowden
Walters Jn. Hy. grocer, Noss Mayo. T N Plymstock 60X6
Wyatt George, assistant overseer, Bridge end

Arthur L. Clamp – the man behind the books

Arthur Leslie Clamp was a man of boundless energy with a passion for helping others, particularly through his love of history. A printer by trade, he started his career in a printing company before moving his family from Exeter to Plymouth to teach at the Plymouth College of Art and Design, where he eventually became the Head of the Printing Department.

Arthur with his five children.

A Devoted Family Man

Despite his love of teaching, Arthur prioritised his family, always making it home by 5:30pm for tea. He and his wife, Rosemary, raised five children: Susan, Angela, Elizabeth, David, and Steven. Arthur would often combine his love of family and history by taking his children on Sunday walks, encouraging them to appreciate historical monuments by taking photos or making crayon rubbings of gravestones for his books. The family home at 203 Elburton Road was a hub of activity, with a large garden, featuring a two-storey fort and a makeshift swimming pool.

A Lifelong Learner and Adventurer

Arthur's thirst for knowledge extended beyond history to a deep curiosity about the world. He was passionate about exploring different cultures, traditions, and cuisines, often taking advantage of his long summer holidays as a teacher to travel to places like India, Russia, South America, the middle east and the USA, sometimes bringing one of his children along. This adventurous spirit even influenced his home life, as seen by the short-lived family tradition of steam-cooking vegetables after a trip to Iceland.

History is a prominent feature of family days out

Community and Philanthropic Spirit

His commitment to serving others was evident in his long-standing involvement with the Elburton Methodist Church. He was the Sunday School Superintendent for over 15 years and served as the editor of the wider church's monthly newsletter, "The Link," for a similar duration. After Rosemary's very sad passing, Arthur later remarried and, following a chance encounter with a professor from India, established a connection with a missionary school in Chennai. Together with his new wife, Christine, he co-founded a "Sponsor a Child's Education" program that continues to this day.

*Pictured left – The cover of 'The Link' complete
with hand drawn sketches of each church by Angela
Below right – Arthur Clamp promoting his latest book
Below left – Arthur at home with his first wife, Rosemary
Below centre – Arthur on holiday with his second wife, Christine*

A Legacy of Learning and Positivity

Arthur's greatest passion was history, which he brought to life through tireless research, documentation, and the many books he authored. He was driven by a need to "never be stuck in a rut," constantly seeking new experiences, meeting new people, and expanding his knowledge. With a positive attitude and a great sense of humour, he was always ready to help others, leaving a lasting impact on his family and community. His children, Susan, Angela, Elizabeth, David, and Steven, remember him with love and gratitude.

David Clamp, 2025

A Legacy of Local History

Below is the story of how Arthur L Clamp began writing books, in his own words, drafted shortly before he passed away in 2001. I have only made minor alterations to this text, correcting grammatical errors that he did not survive to correct himself. When I first discovered this text, I was shocked to see my name mentioned. It seems that, unbeknownst to me, I shared my first PC with him. I suspect he used it during the day when I was at school, although I do have one memory of sitting with him and showing him how it worked. It has been a pleasure to pick up where he left off and see his books republished and redistributed, and to know that I was part of the story, even back then. It was also fascinating to discover that his pricing structure matches the way I have tried to price the books, with a third going to local sellers and the rest covering printing costs with a little left over for my expenses.

I am his eldest grandson, and it is a privilege to curate his legacy, which we are calling 'The Clamp Collection'. The very last line of the text originally reads "The following pages list all the titles." Sadly, that page is missing and we have no record of all the books he published and knowing that some of those were researched by other authors makes the process of finding them even harder. I look forward to one day completing the collection and seeing them all available again. And maybe, one day, I'll even start writing my own to add to the series. For now, here is his story in his own words.

Steven Gibson, 2025

Writing and Publishing Booklets on Local Topics and Areas

I started this interest in either 1968 or 1969 when living in Woodford. I had by these dates established the Department of Printing and I think I must have been looking for something different to do. The first titles were of A5 size proofed from type set at Clarke, Doble and Brendon, Ltd., Plymouth printers, and then made up into pages and printed at Sawtell and Neilson, Ltd., Totnes.

Then began a slow process of getting them out to shops, etc. which proved to be more time consuming and difficult than actually researching, writing and getting the books into print. However, I persisted and opened a business account with Barclays Bank on the Broadway. I was advised to give it a title so I called it "Westway Publications". There came along another problem, one of storage of paper and finished books which was solved when the family moved to Elburton in 1970.

I changed the printer to Penwell, Ltd., Callington, Cornwall, as he was then just setting up himself and his prices seemed very reasonable. I did not get any of the printers to make up the complete books. I hand folded the flat printed sheets, stitched the books on a small manual table stitcher and trimmed them in a small hand turned guillotine which I bought from someone in Penzance for £40. It was brought up in a van.

The trouble and time going to and fro to Callington was too much so I transferred the printing to PDS Printers, Prince Rock, Plymouth, and I have been with them ever since. Now they are at Plympton which is easy to reach and they fold the flat sheets which was turning out to be a long chore which only saved a small part of the printing costs.

All my first titles were written by myself. I took the photographs and developed them in the loft of the house, the type was set by now on a computer situated in the house at Elburton from which I had collected photographic lengths of text to cut up and law down as pages.

At some point I decided that I would do my own film processing of lith film so I bought a large second hand process camera from Kingsbridge and learnt through trial and error to make line negatives of the text and halftone negatives of the illustrations which proved more difficult than I anticipated. The main problem was trying to keep the developer in the large dish at the correct temperature as any change would affect the developing time. I replaced this old camera with a brand new one bought from Croydon, Surrey, costing £900. This has turned out to be a great asset cutting out an expensive part of the printer's costs and one crucial aspect of the work which I could control.

By the middle 1970s there were many outlets I had contacted in Plymouth, up to Dartmoor, Exeter, around to Torbay, Totnes, Dartmouth and the South Hams. The market for local books was much greater than I had first thought and through getting to know many local people undertaking research themselves had the chance to help and make up books for other people who had in most instances, got together a collection of photographs with some text in a rather muddled way. Through my experience in print I was able to shape up their work and get it into print and in every case I had to pay the printer and let the person have the royalties. In the majority of titles produced in this manner this was another way of producing titles and it did give some profit to my work. However, I must say that in a few cases I lost out by either the other person getting the numbers wrong, not returning any monies from stock I delivered or they thought that more of their books should have been sold.

The print run was usually 1,000 copies and from time to time I have had reprints of 250 copies. It took about ten years to clear the first print run so I always had large stocks in the garage, workshop, etc. The numbers sold during the early years was about 7,000 copies a year increasing to around 9,000 copies and for the whole of the enterprise about 500,000 have been sold. The booklets have become part of the local scene and many people collect them, shops regularly order copies and I go around certain areas month by month restocking or replacing titles as necessary.

During the past year or so I have started setting the text on a Packard Bell PC, something which I should have done some years back. I share it with Steven Gibson, my grandson. There appears to be no end to the market for local books, but I could not earn a regular income because of the long time it takes to sell stock.

However, now exceeding 100 titles made up mainly of A4 twenty-four page booklets, some folded guides, with selling prices set with a third going to the shop which is the trade custom, the original idea has been quite successful and could go on for ever.

Apart from monetary benefits, however spasmodically these might be, I have learnt a lot myself, met many interesting people and have become part of the local scene with requests to give talks and to advise people about getting into print.

Arthur L Clamp, 2001

This newspaper article, published by the Evening Herald on 17th August 2001, forms a good record of his life. Just as he encourages us to learn more about local history, we encourage you to learn a little about him. For that reason, we have included these pages at the back of all the most recently republished books, in honour of his memory and recognition of his contribution to the community.

www.ingramcontent.com/pod-product-compliance
Lightning Source LLC
Chambersburg PA
CBHW061407070526
44584CB00031B/4183